Agnese Baruzzi

FIND ME!

Adventures in the Sky

Play along to
sharpen your vision
and mind

FLYING
WOLVES!

Bernard was worried. The young wolf did not see well without his glasses. He thought the glasses made him less scary. Everyone knows wolves are supposed to be scary.

Bernard's three friends had shown him that he could see better when he wore his glasses. He had used them to find lots of things in the forest, in the sea, and underground. He had fun with his friends, but Bernard was very tired now. He wanted peace and quiet. His only wish was to stay at home and be with his friends.

Since Bernard was a wolf, he had to obey the leader of his pack. "We are mighty wolves," the pack leader howled. "We must make everyone afraid of us!"

The leader did not want the wolves to rest and stay at home. "We should be the kings of the world! We must hunt and scare in a new land." Bernard was a little scared himself. What crazy plan would the leader think of next?

He did not have to wait long to find out. The pack leader soon let the wolves hear his big, new plan.

"I just heard from my friend Dingo. He told me about a huge island across the ocean called Australia. It has lots of food and places to explore!" he said.

"There's only one small problem," he added. "Getting to Australia will not be easy. But we can do it! We will travel in airplanes, gliders, and hot-air balloons. We will fly across the ocean!" the pack leader boomed.

Bernard was very unhappy. He did not think that wolves should fly anywhere. He really did not want to cross an ocean. He just wanted to stay home. But more bad news was coming for Bernard.

"I have goggles for each of you,"
the pack leader explained, passing them out to the wolves. "You will need them to keep bugs and dust out of your eyes when we fly."

Bernard thought he might faint! Another big pair of glasses to wear? This was terrible. How could he see through thick, dirty goggles over his glasses? Plus he would be high in the air and far from home.

Then he heard a little voice. "It will be all right, you'll see! My name is Enrico. With these wings, I have no trouble traveling in the air. Don't worry! I will teach you to see lots of things in the sky. If you follow my directions, by the time we're in Australia, your eyes will be as sharp as an eagle's!"

Bernard was still a little worried, but his new friend encouraged him.

"Are you ready for takeoff?"

One of these hot-air balloons has a hole in it. Which one?

A child has lost something. What is it?

There's something here that doesn't belong. Can you see what it is?

Look how many colors there are! 2 of these balloons are the same. Can you find them?

The ducks are migrating south! 3 of them are offering a ride to friends who also want to migrate. Find them!

Look for the pairs!
Each airship on the left page
has a twin on the right page.
Find them!

So many colorful butterflies! Find the one butterfly that doesn't look like any of the others.

Bernard discovers
that there's life in space!
But there are 3 animals
who don't live here.
Find them!

Of all these birds,
there is only one who does
not know how to fly.
Who is it?

There's a fire! Find it!

Look for something to help put out the fire.

Someone is out of place here!

6 twin sets of airplanes are flying over the airport. There is a small difference between the planes in each pair. Find all 6 differences!

There are 5 owls going to a pajama party. Find them!

In the sky, many colorful skydivers can be seen. Only 2 of them look the same. Find them!

Find 6 blue flags.

Can you see a blue T-shirt?

Do you see a swallow's nest?

The 2 tall skyscrapers look the same, but they have 10 differences. Find them!

Birds of all colors live in the jungle. There are 2 of each kind that are the same. Find the pairs!

One alien has a cold. Which one?

Find the slithery outsider here.

Can you find 3 yellow rockets?

Many strange aliens are floating around in space. Only 3 are unlike any of the others. Find them!

Do you see the lazy acrobat?

A strange creature has escaped from the circus. Where is it?

Find something odd that does not belong here.

Luna Park has
2 Ferris wheels that
are almost identical!
Find the 10 differences
between them.

5 flamingos in this flock
are having a snack.
Find them!

Someone is in danger! Who?

Find the tropical bird.

There's something out of place here. Find it!

Each helicopter on the left page has a twin helicopter on the right page. Each pair is different in some way! Find the 12 differences.

Sydney's sky is lit up with colorful fireworks. Welcome to Australia! Which firework is different from the rest?

Did you correctly answer all the questions?

FIND OUT HERE!

You will find the solutions
to all the games on the next few pages.
Check your powers of observation
and decide if you need to go back
and repeat the exercise!

You will see that some solutions have:

★ A star to show the characters in the main
game and in the special questions.

④ Numbers to help you check if you have
found all the animal pairs.

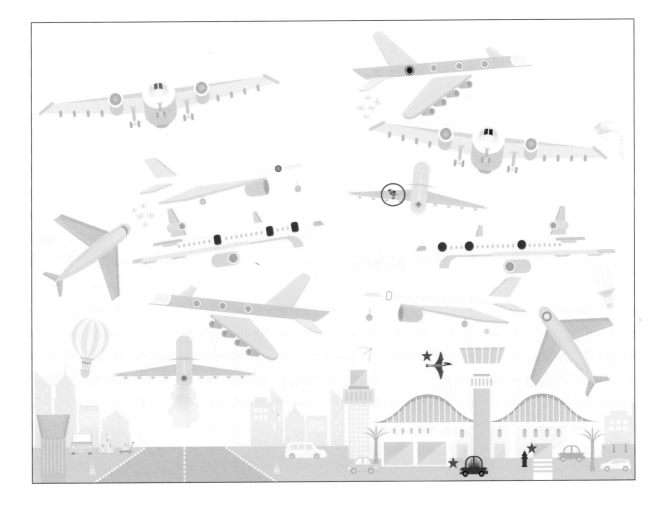

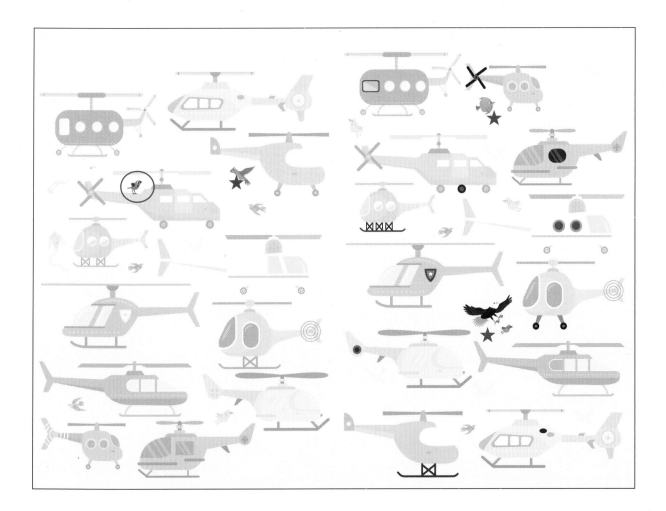

Agnese Baruzzi

Born in 1980, Agnese Baruzzi has a degree in Graphic Design from the Higher Institute for Artistic Industries in Urbino, Italy. Since 2011, she has been working as an illustrator and author of children's books in Italy, the United Kingdom, Japan, Portugal, the United States, France, and Korea. She organizes workshops for children and adults in schools and libraries, and collaborates with agencies, graphic design studios, and publishers. In the last few years, Agnese has illustrated several books for White Star Kids and Happy Fox Books, including *Find Me! Adventures Underground*, *Find Me! Adventures in the Forest*, and *Find Me! Adventures in the Ocean.*

White Star Kids® is a registered trademark property of White Star s.r.l.

© 2020 White Star s.r.l.
Piazzale Luigi Cadorna,
6 20123 Milan, Italy
www.whitestar.it

All rights reserved. No part of this publication may be reproduced, stored in a retrieval system, or transmitted in any form or by any means, electronic, mechanical, photocopying, recording, or otherwise, without written permission from the publisher.

Translation: Megan Bredeson; Editing: Phillip Gaskill

Originally published as *Find Me! Adventures in the Sky with Bernard the Wolf* by White Star, this North American version titled *Find Me! Adventures in the Sky* is published in 2020 by Fox Chapel Publishing Company, Inc. Reproduction of its contents is strictly prohibited without written permission from the rights holder.

Happy Fox Books is an imprint of Fox Chapel Publishing Company, Inc., *www.FoxChapelPublishing.com*, 903 Square Street, Mount Joy, PA 17552.

ISBN 978-1-64124-062-8 (Hardcover)
ISBN 978-1-64124-115-1 (Paperback)
Library of Congress Control Number: 2020935091

We are always looking for talented authors. To submit an idea, please send a brief inquiry to acquisitions@foxchapelpublishing.com.

Fox Chapel Publishing makes every effort to use environmentally friendly paper for printing.

Printed in China